A Way of Knowing

WRS

A WAY OF KNOWING

Collected Poems
1970–2020

William R. Stott, Jr.

Edited by Paul J. McCarren, S.J.

NEW ACADEMIA PUBLISHING   SCARITH

Washington, DC

Library of Congress Control Number: 2020923803
ISBN 978-1-7348659-3-6 (alk. paper)

SCARITH   An imprint of New Academia Publishing

New Academia Publishing
4401-A Connecticut Avenue NW #236, Washington DC 20008
info@newacademia.com - www.newacademia.com

NEW ACADEMIA
PUBLISHING

For the Father
now and all ways
for all days,
my thanks always.

For my Father
who with
hands and heart
showed me how.

For the privileged
state of Fatherhood
praise and wonder
always.

Contents

Editor's Note

I met Bill Stott in 1974 at Fordham University when we taught Shakespeare by directing students to put the plays on their feet. Bill could teach students the actor's discipline of reacting directly to what you're seeing and hearing because it's the same discipline he practices as a poet. He says his work as a poet is to describe what he observes, creating an image that's "concrete, specific, palpable, and real." How do you come to know what's going on around you? Observe—that is, watch, listen; watch and listen some more; then say what you've observed. You can re-create this experiment in epistemology if you read Bill's poems aloud. Savor them as an actor savors a dramatic monologue; let the words pulse into life.

It's difficult to contemplate what we're experiencing; judgment is always jumping in: "Oh, I see what that is. OK. Next." We tend to be like the White Rabbit in *Alice in Wonderland*—rushing on to next with no time for now. A poet does the opposite, asking: "Wait; what's that; what's it doing; what's causing that sound—that smell?" The poet has learned to linger, to watch as things unfold. The poet measures time with love, not with efficiency, and shares that love with readers who are willing to enter a moment and abide a while.

When I asked Bill what inspired him to collect these poems now (some of them were first published in the '70s and '80s), he said he took them out recently, recollecting many of them as first drafts, or as notes for further fiddling. But as he read them, he was surprised to find them finished. They came alive again in a surprising way. Now he wants to let them loose so he can move on to more looking and listening.

Paul J. McCarren, S.J.

Losing, Gaining

Van Gogh

Whose gold fixed the sun
on the buzzing burning hill,
     Walked
Because—after her fashion—
The goddess loved him
     Behind her eyes:
Seeing there what he couldn't see
In the shock-still streets
     Until
That certain time, when
Singed by searing light
     They ran
And running drowned
His violent end.

8 December 1962

The old men sit on benches, coldly blue,
Shaped by a wan but detonating sun,
Wrinkled and frayed and phallically rue,
They preside over clean-picked carrion.
Others, all hunched shoulder and averted eye,
—Wooden glances in a wind forced freeze—
Marionette now swiftly by,
Their shadows flicked with mechanic ease.
The discharge of day yields an amber flood
That spilling soaks the river's rim
Where a wheeling gull scans the flats of mud
And shrieking, defies the evening's dim.
While my kindled factor, pulsing hard and bright,
Riots in the sack to see tomorrow's light.

For William Carlos Williams

First the thunder—
        standing at the window,
We watch the rain
        of windfall and
                waterdown.

(An old dog, head down
        and swinging in Sandy Hill,
Loping around the
        larger pools,
                lopes on.)

The clustered sky,
        remaining dark,
Sheds its light
        in splintering shots
                that arc

Across the liquid
        burp and gurgle,
Arching and tickling
        the recumbent ear
                beneath the roar
(A young girl,
        brows pinched in the
Mirror, applies
        to her half-own self some
                light.)

Half understood;
        providing that music
For the living not
        the dead and
                because

(An old man with a
         newspaper on his head,
From store door to store door
         skitters down
               the street.)

This happens every several days
         it will endure,
And you continue
         in Paterson,
               for praise.

Insinuating the world of noon,
I stand
And my sitting blood rebels,
Causing vertigo,
A humming swarm
Of golden green
Distinctly seen
And felt.

Here, on the summit of the day,
Nothing moves
But down the fulcrum's flank
Towards a
Shadowed light,
This noon in slipping,
Shapes
the ruthful night.

SUMMER SHOWER

First the old fierceness,
Sun,
Blisters the tar
In the playground
Where children's cries
And random runs
Bear witness to
The clouded press
Looming in the west;
And in the heated light
They'll wait and meet
The first implosions
O sizzling rain
With chaotic glee;
Beading up
And bunching
And running,
Surrounding themselves
—Totally absorbed—
In their own
Collisions.

Ars Moriendi

The chatter, squeal and squeak of hempen rigging,
Sailor set;
The breeze-rippled crispness
of a sweet spring morning;
Breath-blown shouts;
In the pale new sun
And the fresh white light,
A setting now into patterned grunts;
A heave, a shout, a heave,
A sudden sand-sucked scrape,
The sweeps catch hold.
A thrust . . . Underway!
Deep in effort, the sailors only dimly hear
Children's cries and women's wails
Grow thin and wanly fade
In the wind.
> A furore Normanorum
> Libera nos Domine.

Skirting beaked headlands,
The long-necked ship,
Eagle-ready,
Flies over shadowed water.
Harald Hardraada, he of the hard rule,
Sternly stands
And scans the set of sail,
The wind-snapped canopy,
The great shields and sharp spearpoints.
In the growing colored day,
All flushed with gold.
The ship's a thing of ease
In the folding green,
Cutting through its constant clasp,
The sea hisses past swelling strakes,
Roils from stem to skeg.
> A furore Normanorum
> Libera nos Domine.

A skein of geese tangle
In an air tossed cloud.
Now in the open sea,
The wind fetches chop.
Her neck all foam.
She creaks and groans, heaves and plunges.
The sail snaps and swells,
Cracks and catches
The inconstant gust.
The sinking sun
Wets the surge with blooded light.
Arms ache and sweat chills.
A pelting spray seasons the gnawed cold meat.
Fey Hardraada, he of the hard rule,
Is ruddy
And bloody in the rich red light.

A furore Normanorum
Libera nos Domine.

The billow and roar of wind and sea
In a light-fraught darkness,
Eyes widen and
Voices hush in
The brazier's flickering flame.
Night comes down,
All black down save
Some far grey gleams.
A voice raises to set and secure.
The whipping wind wracks
The heave and the wrench.
The sunstone's set aside for the lack of the light.
In the furious dark
Fey Hardraada, he of the hard rule,
Shoulders set,
Stares eagerly ahead.

A furore Normanorum
Libera nos Domine.

IN OTHER WORDS

ENCOUNTER

Just after morning stars,
In a galvanic light.
I watched him watching,
Measuring this bow-split wave
By shutting alternately.
One eye, then the other,
Rocking in a heel to toe antiphony
On a metronomic sea.

Just after morning stars,
In a galvanic light,
I watched him watching
A gull—mounted on the early sun—
Slip into a flooding river of
Wind, while over his heavy
Fist, a tuneless whistle missed
The song.

Just after morning stars,
In this galvanic light,
I watched him watching
Me.

I was reading in *Time* magazine today
About a psychological ofay
By the name of Mr. Rollo May
Who uses existential therapy
And a sense of death as necessary
If the healed and happy life's to be.

My woman's out hustling a streetcorner punk
As I sit in our rat-bitten room.
I'm way down in a deep blue funk
And damn well feel a sense of doom.
If a sense of death's an aching lack
Often associated with being black,

Then I'll no longer feel any strife
But render thanks to Mr. Rollo May
Whose philosophy has shown me life
In those bitter feelings I used to wish away.
For black makes white, a whore's a wife,
And best of all from death comes life.

ORDINANDUS

Clean ribbed and slim hipped, He rises
And thoroughly washes in the clean dawn.
Give virtue to my hands, O Lord,
That I may serve without defilement.
To be sure, there is certain and solemn assistance,
The vestments neatly laid out,
The dignity enormous.

In silence made more silent
For the well-oiled hum,
They, with the assurance borne of practice,
Helped him with the liquid-cooled
Undergarment. Its tubed tracery
Touches and reminds his skin.
Cleanse me, O Lord, and purify my heart.

Mime-like, they move and minister,
Suggesting something greater than grace.
The pressure garment, slack and
Flaccid now, is next. Gird me,
O Lord, with the girdle of Purity
And extinguish in my loins
The bite of lust.

Electronic checks and balances.
In this antiseptic place, pulsing readouts
Accompany the assumption of
The micrometeoroid protection garment;
Its lightweight materials heavy in sum.
May I be worthy, O Lord,
To receive the reward of my labor.

Silent and studious, they pat
And adjust the thermal overgarment,
Its white synthetic skin impresses
With the illusion of completeness

And congruence.
Restore to me, O lord, the stole
Of immortality for transgressions taken.

With muted voices and a time check,
The preparation moves to its end.
With a final silent wish,
The helmet is secured in place.
Place, O Lord, the helmet of salvation
On my head, that I may overcome
The assaults of the devil.

He moves now, weighted
And a bit unreal,
Through well-lubricated doors,
Down silent passageways.
As I draw near your sacred
Mystery, may I be found worthy
Of everlasting joy.

He moves now, weighted
And a bit unreal,
Towards the galactically extreme;
Towards a beginning in the sun,
By the sun, with the sun.
Beati qui non viderunt
Et crediderunt.

FEELEY AND GRIFFIN'S

Out of the sun, through the entry and
Into the cave they come,
Noses wrinkled at the beery stale.
Soon eyes dilate to the darkness,
A kind of academy brown.
The stained and bruised old bar
Stands, strong in siege.
Now behind, the sun beats itself
Pale against the smoky pane.
It's not needed now.

Here they are, the hard handed young
Whose laughter, coughs and curses nicely
Balance, in stressed debate
Or high-pitched put-on.
Here they are, the ladies,
Effete and wrung.
Large in their efforts at dignity,
And fat with letting go,
They indicate their progress
With an extended pinky.

Here he is. Huddled in a corner,
The gnarled monologist carries on.
Eyes wildly alive,
Hands casting broken thought,
His mumbling dribbles to a grizzled chin.
Here they are. Time-twisted old men
Whisper viciously . . . and longingly
Into borrowed ears

As if the whispered hiss
Will raise the yellow leaf.
Here am I, relishing the thick cool
Stout, the acrid scratch of flame,
The swallowed bite of smoke.
Here am I, relishing replication and
The time to watch a curiously
Still point in time.
Here we are, all in the cave,
Huddled shards but not unnecessary.
The ligature only as intense as the need;
A shriving time allowed.

In the Prado

I

Have you ever seen Bosch's great triptych?
Do you know the one I mean?
It's over here . . . how strange and sad it is.
It's called "The Garden of Earthly Delights."
The old masters had a sure sense of sin.
In Eden even there are hints for the
Control seems precarious and the whole scene
Urgent. Admittedly, there's a certain
Grave arrest of tails and wings and surge;
But look, the antennaed hills, remote against
A milk blue sky, loom behind a golden
Turret, shot through with the swirl of dark birds.
Muted meadows and emblematic beast
Overlook a pond that is thick with life,
A pond pierced by a pink fount of complex
Form with, see, a hole in its egg-shaped base.
True, it dominates, but at its lower
Edge, crawling things emerge while on the upper
Rim — by the mustard colored meadow —
Those that walk, drink at the water's edge.
Tails, wings and beaks are present but quiet.
See here, central in the early light, Christ
Looks away towards, well, who knows what.
He seems troubled and concerned or at least
As if he knows something. Over there, on
His right, that tree seems almost obscene, it's
So swollen, but fascinating as well.
There's Adam, sitting low, but looking up
At Christ while Eve, kneeling higher and touched
By Christ's left hand, looks down demurely;
Or is it at the busy animals
In and around yet another pond?
Here in the very morning of things
All seems quite silent but a bit ominous,
The calm is touched by a sense of hazard.

II

Over to the right in the central panel,
Which is really "The Garden" itself,
—It's as gay as anything he painted—
The forms are round, swollen, almost bloated.
Note how the play here is on the circle
And the so-called alchemical world egg.
Against the pale milky sky there is much
Busyness. Wildly festooned erections
Dominate but those steel-colored shapes
Are also formidable, even a
Bit frightening with their sword-like bristles.
Just below, a more or less normal
Correlation between beast and man is
Maintained as they circle ceaselessly
Around and around a body of water.
They appear to be herding . . . or herded.
A bit lower, in front of a thorned and
Fruity hedge—really a line of demarcation—
Birds are larger than men and the sight
Is strange if not sinister. Look at all
The people here. Intertwined and grasping,
Reaching and touching, they reveal all the
Lineaments of desire. One can see,
In a most delicate and curiously
Abstracted way, all the permutations
And combinations of flesh to flesh.
One easily understands the avid
Glance, the lascivious clasp, the frank and
Almost charming concupiscence.
The moving water is engorged with life.
Do you hear anything? Perhaps it's odd
But I always have the sense of sound in
The garden, shivering, high-pitched and pervasive.
Our ganglia are tickled by a feverish rhythm
As if the music were made by tuning forks.
In any case, see that in spite of the

Fact that everyone is doing—or done
With doing—something to someone,
How insular and isolated they are.
Here, his symbols are marshaled in ornate
Dance: the observant owls, for instance,
Time-honored emblems of heresy, note the
Translucent and separate elements
Of the circle. Grapes, cherries, strawberries.
Dribbling seed pods, the fruits of love are all
Here in recipe to charge the scene,
To make it heated, aphrodisian.
Lower down, in the left quadrant, yes, there,
The floating bubble with the couple in it?
It depicts alchemical marriage
I find it most disquieting.
The look on her face is somehow detached,
Suggestive of something else as if she
Hears an echo or sees another sight.
In the lower field, filled with flesh,
The bodies compose a luxurious arabesque
Of tortured but curiously abstract
Proportion. People though . . . yearning and straining . . .
Incessant. Think of it! How deceitful
Lust is. In the intensity of the itch,
It promises everything and then . . . again and again.
The fragile style of these denizens
Is accentuated and threatened by
Thorny thickets, jagged rocks and sharp beaks.
All of the frenzy can neither blind nor
Obscure the sense of grievous distraction,
The sense of something remembered.
The desires, though artful, are still fevered
And not lasting. It's almost, in fact, as if
They don't really know what they're doing.

III

The Hell, as you might well expect, isn't
Very pretty but it is gripping.
A spectral horizon, billowing with flame,
Casts its outline, with shades of gray.
The effect is both lurid and leaden.
See, just below, the acute torture of
The knife ears and of those crushed beneath
That which clearly has heard too much.
The weird and sly pale overseer is next
Whose rather urbane ironic face is text
Enough for surety. His shattered egg-shaped
Torso suggests the missing fragments.
Balanced precariously on blasted branches,
His blanched head in turn balances
A rather puckish brim on which a
Pink bladdered bagpipe spouts smoke. See the
Dancing bird-man march around the brim, with a
Look of idiot glee, oblivious to sin.
To the immediate left of our guide,
We see a slab of skull, bone bare and bleached.
Note the many cutting edges . . . tearers
And rippers . . . and the water seems dark and deep.
Surely here, the sense of sound is clear,
Plangent, metallic, dinning, a screech to
Scrape the inner ear, at least.
In the lower part of the panel, I
See the figures as bound, confused, confined;
Compelled to endless separateness, alive
To constant dying. They are presided
Over by images of music and gaming.
And an enigmatic reptilian insect,
His beak bent—with much tearing, I should think.
In sum, there's a sense of demonic din,
Of atomic misdirection, of shouts
And the flicker of a scream.

RHESUS

Face fixed
In a sardonic grin,
He finishes picking at
The salted certainties of self,
Rises,
And begins to dance
An antic frenzy
On the plated branches
Of his cage.
Slight but vital,
He works wild
In the neon light;
Working to the man's shadowed bulk,
Masked by night.
He works and wakens in his blood,
Fierce fires along his veins.

TRISTESSE

Punctured by light,
The pearly murk now hosts
A wrinkled shadow dance
That moves
To the thinly mournful cries
Of fishermen
Which shiver and excite
The pliant thighs of night.

A quiet wind,
In its borne mist,
Riffles her soft dark wet
—now a half heard murmur—
Touching with its sweep,
Nudged-in prows
Along warped piers and
Sleep.

Here on this lofty eminence
Where eagles scream and the
Silent rushing colorless wind
Blows about,
Far over the low and level sands
That burn away—
We sense the dim and alarms
Where the sea holds sway.

We touch our dry old hands
And looking down
Watch the shadows of the day
Hold our children fixed in play
And feel, well, high away
Almost . . . Olympian,
As we hold hands
And dream of loins now dry
And spay—or fixed
(By time's fine trick).

In a way, we feel sure
That our move
To this high rimmed country
Is a good one.
It's better, after all,
To have been in
That ceaseless butting flux
And having been,
Now free to see
The backward toss
And abysm of time.

I recall the awful delicacy
Of her three quarter inclined head,
fingers shaping the temple
Tendrilled hair; she, so slim
And fair and self-possessed.

Did it begin, was it shaped
In the first tentative touch
Or in the quickly thudding
Blood and/or ended as well
In a rapiered spasm?

At the moment of which,
All outside of self,
One waits the chugging spew
To catch and, in a sense,
Release the fearful involvement.

No real release for we
Now await the day
Of the fetching forth of flesh.
Extruded and defined.

With longing we will pay
For that primal plain
Balanced in the night
And its realized rich delight.

Will we await the day
Locked in by hope of night
Or opt, instead, to play
The price of ruthless light?

A Joy Proposed
A Dream Taken

A sun shot light
Hits the rich dark loam,
Ricochets to shade
Around the fields of home

Creamy rich skin,
A passion loosed face,
Soft thrustings in
A dark and secret place

A sweet short clutch
Exploding into bloom,
Racing the whorl,
Then the coming on down.

Ebbing recedes
Along now nerveless limbs,
Minds start to heed
That memories are dim.

A Touch of Wry

Mr. A. Jason Lockhart made lists
And liked the winter earth,
All brown and loafed and spare.
"One can see," he said, "if not the growth,
The patterns for what they are;
The form of the fields' end, the outline
of twisted trunk, the curve of rivers' edge,
All in icy clarity."
He told of the low pale sun which
Always keeps his plants—through the chilled pane—
As green "as one would want them";
Of the lovely quiet snow blending
All into one grand silence;
Of the winter's roars? "Why, we're
Indoors and understand because
Of all the seasons
Winter's reasons are the most direct.
Oh you'll hear," he said, "people
Speak of death but they miss winter's point,
Death's over.
Here," he blushed, "right here,
Warm and fuzzy with wine,
I find it easy to make love.
It's just," he stretched, "that a man knows
More of what's expected of him in winter.
Its law and order's clear and unconcerned."

Mr. A. Jason Lockhart made lists
And felt uneasy in the summer.
"The blown and colored earth is nice
Enough, the gleams and shaded light.
But it's hard
To see where one ends
And the other begins.
The sight of shifting golds
And thick dense greens"—he frowned—
"Too much seen.
Listen," he said, "the sounds are loud,

Barks, chirps, hisses, a constant
Humming drone in the sun.
Really, a kind of tumult
And shouting—a man can't think—
And why? Why all the folding and overlapping?
Life?
Listen, there's a lot of killing here.
Life's death to be done."
He paused, "Much wetness and . . . dilation,
Opening into folds and . . . colors, down
Inner . . . secret parts.
That's it! Dilation and secretion.
I don't know. I guess
I dislike the illusion of concern
In the heated summer sky."

The room is electric,
Pulsing and loud
As the drum's frantic roll
Quiets the crowd.

                    Aretha,
                    Oh yea.

With skin of brown satin
And a bloody red voice,
The syncopated wail
Paralyzes choice.

                    Aretha,
                    Oh yea.

She's dappled by neon,
Sequined by light,
And with shudders of pain
Enriches the night.

                    Aretha,
                    Oh, yea.

She sings from the bowels
Concerning the soul
And overwhelms the past
By blessing the toll.

                    Aretha,
                    Oh, yea.

Haiku

Children on the lawn
Last as long as sparrows who
Are unoptioned too.

The biggest difference
(from *Family Weekly*, March 19, 1972)

True—
according to psychological studies
at Aberdeen,

the biggest difference between
men and women
was in the way
they regarded Envy and Lust.

Women rated Envy the worst,
men put it in third place.
As for Lust, women ranked it well
up the list, above
Anger, Sloth and Gluttony while
men ranked it least
reprehensible.

The biggest difference between
men and women
was in the way
they regarded Envy and Lust,

according to psychological studies
at Aberdeen,
True—

ON THE POINT

"Ich bin wie eine Fahne von Fernen umgeben ... "
—Rainer Maria Rilke

I am an Ensign given over to deep space
To predict the gathering storms;
But I am to live through them
By letting them blow beneath me.
Below, things do not move:
Oaks stand straight, stairs don't creek,
Doors are silent on their sills,
Dust sits and windows wait
While chimneys fill with smoke.

Then I feel storms shake the sea
And the sea shake the beach.
My order is given to spread out;
But I fall back to myself
Only then to hurl myself,
Sighted and alone,
Into the shaken sea.

Epigram
(written after a visit to a "residential" nursing home)

Recognize what it is the aged hate:
The less time they have; the more they wait.

A Suite
of Epiphanies

THE TOP OF MY SON

Sitting in the kitchen in my skivvies,
A little bit drunk on the linoleum floor,
Having a post-prandial, pre-Morphean tin
—Feeling thoroughly mortal and full of sin—
I root through the children's Christmas toys
And find the top of my son, a modern
Scientific one: "A Whizzer," the box says,
"Of infinite gyroscopic possibilities."

It's a round plastic ball from the bottom
Of which a metal tip protrudes. I weigh
The cool pink shape and thrust, rolling the tip,
Leaning hard and harder, making low-grade
Gray marks on the newly scrubbed floor.
Velocity increases in proportion
To pressure in accordance with the law.
It warms and hums and quickens in my hand.

With great expectation, I gingerly
Set the top down. After one sharp skip it
Finds the ground point and then sings a music
Sweet to the inner ear, a music of
Balance, explicability and sense.
Blur-swollen, penultimate and sure,
Its precise song and dance is heard and seen
Only by me—now rapt in a cosmic trance.

My folded leg cramps and the reflex jerk
Touches the top. It starts and begins to
Wobble and shudder on a now erratic
Tip. Its last spasms are gross till it finally
Flops, skittering out of my reach.
My eyes sting and I swallow very hard.
Sitting in the kitchen in my skivvies,
A little bit drunk on the linoleum floor.

County Park

Last night there was a savage ice storm,
Still the pond is not yet frozen;
Indeed, the day seems rather warm.
Only the sound of shedding ice
Provides an index, faint but nice,
To the depth of the exhausted quiet.
Suddenly, over the arthritic trees,
I hear the honk, then see the geese.
Washing their wings in the soapy sky,
They soon skim in to rinse in gray water.
Back from the pond in a gravel lot,
A rusty Falcon scrapes to a stop
And an old man with bread emerges.
I know him from town. He lives alone,
Saves string, newspapers, bits of junk;
In fact, anything against the day.
He shuffles to the dull brown verge
And braces to meet the squabbling surge
Of gluttonous but knowledgeable birds.
Battling and gaggling, ducks and geese
Flock forward. Pecky and nervous,
They clutch round him. He doesn't seem
Particularly pleased to see them and
Speaks with some fury—in a rasping
Whisky tenor—while he feeds. They answer
With cranky asthmatic croaks.
One, a Mallard, in a breaded frenzy,
Nips him on the rump and he curses and kicks
The ingrate away. With an ungainly
Wobble and a petulant quack, the
Offender makes his way to the back to
Begin again. In all, a noisy
Community in an atonal feast,
Resonant with echoes of ecology.

The Morning after the Ice Storm

Is as relevant
As the sun smudged sky,
The tree traced ice,
Croaking geese just past,
The sugar spiked grass,
The world frozen fast,
Ducks taking to task
My missing Mass—
just that—
No more . . . no less.

PENELOPE

In the early morning bed,
Molded by body prints
And touched by special smells,
Hallowed in the hollow of my arms
My naked playful son
Touches me and grins.
I look long at him and he at me
And we talk: of the first,
The biggest, the most.
Lying on my chest, he
Rubs my beard and pulls my hair.
He likes that and I
his lean self.
Soon it will be time to rise,
To shave,
To be diminished by dress,
Then, he'll sense the lack of specialness
And begin to ask
Ithakan questions.

Bottom Dreaming

Well, it's honest employment and true,
As sure as houses and almost as safe,
For all must be dressed, however roughly,
At least since cast from the God damned garden.
Such thoughts though, are for a little moment
And even now are remanded to the thick fingers
That work the humming loom and shed warped
Patterns of light, but patterns that soon will
Yield suggestions beyond pattern, at least
To the unfixed point of reverie. The
Drone now noises at the edge of this light,
Nibbles at the web of dream, or memory.
Not unlike the tangled hill beyond the room
Whose leafed shadows support and hold the sky.

As quiet as an eyelid and as quick,
He's moved to the unravelling dream. Here,
no roughly loomed cloth will do. He now has
An emperor's clothes, new and simply rich.
Some facts can neither be denied nor ignored
And in the sweet dark wood he was one who
Saw and smelled, heard and felt all there was.
His eyes glaze in sensual astonishment.
Again he is quite taken with the song
And the stroking but in course the whistling
Causes a recollective shiver for
He's never far from flesh. His belly
Rumbles and he checks the height of the sun.
At the very least, that is done and well.

GOING

We leave off cutting down the weeds
And taking up the ceaseless green.
Redressed, we make ready to go
And then, when we get there,
Are strangely stunned
By the fixed realities of stone and glass;
But soon we go in
And pass in silent files
To sit and witness the procession
Of nodding flower faced children.
Their motion and rustle
Soon settle into seats, neat in rows,
All brave in their brightness.
He's there, and we can see him,
Grave in his sense of center,
Blithe in his ignorance of the ragged edge.
My unease becomes resentment
As I brood over his breeding,
Sullen that I should have to bite
The bitter bread of his mortality
And the fact that his days,
Told in this way,
Sun me into shadow.
Soon we will rise and go to share
So he can go a progress through
The guts of my begging that it
Is he who's really there.

Reading the Signs

"Can a poet imagine a sequence that is devoid
of any passing of time, when the poem shifts
from space to space, point to point, as long as
there are more than two points on the diagram?"
— Angus Fletcher

Digging was what he did, what he had done:
Year after year in the squinting light and wind.
Lately, he sensed a meaning in the sum
Although he paid it no special mind.
But soon — and sure — he knew the time had come.
He cast the entrailed earth to understand
And read the still designs, to no avail.

Next morning (his name for it) he stayed in bed
And heard the talk about his shirking.
He turned his back to her and what she said:
"You never gave a damn about your work."
Tossing her head she went to spin the day;
Surprised, for she was used to winning
Ever since the very beginning.

Day after day, in the aching stricken light,
He didn't dig; he perfected his stare.
Even the suffocating dark of night
Saw him wholly disposed to be aware.
Then he arose and, armed with a wand,
Sectioned the sky in a series of arcs.
Watching, she asked by eye; "practice," he said.
Finally he got around to the sun.
It was behind him, over in the west,
Back toward the past from where they had come.
He gathered himself in a circle he'd pressed
Into the dust. Huge and naked he sat
(he refused to dress) staring at the sky;
And felt bitter relief when the crow flew by.

49

A Suite
of Journey Poems

SUITE

FROM DAMASCUS . . .

"Nay, stand thou back; I will not budge a foot.
This be Damascus, be thou cursed Cain,
To slay thy brother Abel if thou wilt."
                              —Shakespeare, *Henry VI*

I

Is it the child's cry
that causes dawn to come,
rosy and cool, breezeless and clear?
Deceived in sleep,
she wakens and—whispering—
moves to feed the insistent maw,
acknowledging
with ever renewable awe,
the crying
on the road from Damascus.

II

Under the oak's huge shade,
on a hazy and
yellow mingled morning,
secrets as dark and deep as blood
are traded and retraded
by boys
with bright assurance.
Pacted and responsible,
they run out
on the road from Damascus.

III

Having danced
an elaborate dalliance
around their stressed and knotted guts,
they sit, still
swollen by hint and touch.
Ritually taut and
exhausted with longing
trembling on this wet summer night—
they barter
on the road from Damascus.

IV

A thinking man's son
invests in the city where
the makers of context
are made.
To spend soft trusts
and get concrete results,
to daub the big wars in conflicting hues,
to realize the worth of others' views
as they deal
on the road from Damascus.

V

He has eyes as rich as wine
and her hair, like wheat
gathered in by the blooming night.
Again, likenesses
being what they are,
a man does well
to call and call for sight
of what it is to be
moving
on the road from Damascus.

VI

In the edged and falling air,
the smell of burning leaves
is fanned incense enough
for the sacrifice of kind inside,
where
the rough cut of confidences,
used and re-used, is shared.
Too true to be common,
contention
on the road from Damascus.

VII

Notwithstanding,
morning dreams do come true,
felt the seer,
his old self straining,
staring into the cold and quiet night,
thinking thermal thoughts
with circular tracings around remembered suns,
listening for the shadows,
stumbling
on the road from Damascus.

Additional Editor's Notes

In preparing this collection, Bill and I had time to talk—and ask Ithakan questions—about each of the poems. A complete record would fill up another book. These notes are a severely edited selection of our back and forth about the following titles.

"Van Gogh"
—Paul J. McCarren: This poem's shape on the page resembles a barely balanced column.
—William R. Stott: It's a run-on—enjambment—like Van Gogh's life running into chaos.

"8 December 1962"
—PJM: Although this is a strict Petrarchan sonnet, its precise form barely keeps its emotional tumult in check.
—WRS: Yes!

"For William Carlos Williams"
—PJM: A brief tour of William Carlos Williams's Paterson?
—WRS: Yes, there's the park [Sandy Hill], Paterson's sleeping giant ["beneath the roar"]; but it's also a praise song—it's a psalm.

"Insinuating the world of noon"
—PJM: I hear many voices in this poem, capturing many moments in various light.
—WRS: There's a jostling of light and time.

"Summer Shower"
—PJM: The shower and the children act almost as one.
—WRS: Drops pooling and flooding together.

"Ars Moriendi"
—PJM: Harald seems to know he's facing death, yet off he sails.
—WRS: He takes his time; time doesn't take him.
—PJM: Did people fear Harald as "furore Normanorum"—the fury and wrath of the Norsemen?
—WRS: "Deliver us from the ravages of the Norsemen" was a

common refrain in the Latin liturgy of the eleventh century. But Harald's love of life was stout even facing defeat and death.

"Encounter"
—PJM: I see a sailor absorbed, reflective, and startled—all in a moment.
—WRS: He's completely caught up in the act of knowing: reflecting—and reflecting on—the moment

"I was reading in *Time* magazine today"
Written after reading a June 1970 issue of *Time* magazine.
—PJM: This fellow's a bit rough on those who "explain" things to us.
—WRS: Too sardonic?

"Ordinandus"
—PJM: This "ordinandus" is being ordained and vested to preside over his own lifting up.
—WRS: Exactly right.

"In the Prado"
During a 1995 trip to Spain, Bill visited the Prado museum and was startled by his response to a work he thought he knew well: Hieronymus Bosch's painting, "The Garden of Earthly Delights."
He had a shock of recognition when he read about a similar response in Ben Lerner's 2011 novel, *Leaving the Atocha Station* in which the narrator observes a lone, early-morning visitor to the Prado standing before a painting, then breaking into silent tears. The weeping man composes himself, moves to another room where a second painting provokes more silent tears. After again composing himself, the man moves to "The Garden of Earthly Delights." Lerner writes that the man "considered it calmly, then totally lost his shit."
—PJM: You're the narrator in this poem, I think. You don't "lose it," but you're clearly gripped by what you see.
—WRS: I'm hoping my passion here invites readers into this painting by Bosch so they can be at one with the tryptych.

"Rhesus"
—PJM: Rhesus/*risus*: the monkey looks, we look—I wonder who's smiling at whom.

"Punctured by light"
—PJM: A charged moment.
—WRS: No more, no less.

"Here on this lofty eminence"
—PJM: These are reflections with relish and rue.
—WRS: Just so.

"I recall the awful delicacy"
—PJM: What a wrestling match! Who's winning?
—WRS: Read it again.

"Mr. A. Jason Lockhart made lists"
—PJM: This paints a nice diptych.
—WRS: It's deliberate: two looks adjacent.

"The room is electric"
—PJM: Hot jazz, raw and sexy!
—WRS: Ah!

"The biggest difference"
—PJM: Here's a touch of wry!
—WRS: Cheers!

"On the Point"
—PJM: You pay tribute while having fun.
—WRS: Yes.

"Epigram"
—PJM: Here's the weight of time (pardon the pun) again.

"County Park"
—PJM: Here again, something ordinary catches the deep mystery and magic of a specific place.
—WRS: For more, see "The Morning after the Ice Storm."

"Penelope"
—PJM: Ithakan questions?
—WRS: Yes. The fundamental and highest art: a father and son asking Ithakan questions.

"Bottom Dreaming"
—PJM: *A Midsummer-Night's Dream*, and . . .
—WRS: Ironically, Bottom's the one who "knits up the raveled sleeve of care."

"Reading the Signs"
—PJM: Fletcher seems to suggest one can diagram a poem. In this poem, you just follow a man as he's moved, and lets himself be moved from digging to dreaming and divining, and you let us watch.

"From Damascus"
—PJM: Folk myth sets Cain's slaughter of Abel in Damascus where, later, Saul (Paul) took up the work of an apostle. Whether burning shame or hot zeal drives you forth in life, your slog will likely include such visions as Stott summons in these seven poems.

Publication History

"Insinuating the world of noon." *Four Quarters* 21, no. 2 (January 1972).

"Ars Moriendi." *Thought* 48, no. 190 (Autumn 1973).

"Encounter." *Georgetown University Journal* (Spring 1984).

"Ordinandus." *Chimaera* (February 1972).

"Feeley and Griffin's." *Ball State University Forum* 19, no. 4 (Autumn 1978).

"Rhesus." *Wisconsin Academy Review* 35, no. 2 (March 1989).

"Punctured by light." *Four Quarters* 21, no. 2 (January 1972).

"Here on this lofty eminence." *Cardinal Poetry Quarterly* 6, no. 4 (March 1972).

"Mr. A. Jason Lockhart made lists." *Quoin* (Spring 1974).

"The Top of My Son." *Riverside Quarterly* 5, no. 3 (August 1972).

"Going." *Four Quarters* (Spring 1974).

"Reading the Signs." *Quoin* (Spring 1974).

About the Author

William (Bill) Stott, Jr. is a teacher, poet, artist, renowned ornithologist, college president and professor, and adult education consultant and lecturer. His collegiate background includes being a past president of Ripon College in Wisconsin. He has served as vice president and dean of students at Georgetown University in Washington, DC, and assistant dean of students at Fordham University in New York. Stott has taught college-level courses in the humanities, natural history, biological sciences, poetry, English and American literature, scripture, philosophy, and history.

One of his most important academic creations is "The Power of Story," a comprehensive re-enactment of the entire Catholic canon, taught in eight semesters over a four-year period. Stott has delivered this series five times since its inception in 1999. In addition to scripture, he teaches ornithology and serves as a director on the Boards of the American Birding Association and Chesapeake Bay Environmental Center. Stott is a former principal with the Fairfax Audubon Society (currently the Audubon Society of Northern Virginia) where he designed and executed a full curriculum in natural history studies that included courses in ornithology, ecology, and botany. Completion of the course constituted a certificate as a Master Naturalist. He is a Fellow National of the Explorers Club, an elected position in which fellows must distinguish themselves by contributing to scientific knowledge in the field of geographical exploration.

He holds degrees from Columbia University and Georgetown University, as well as honorary degrees from Fisk University and Georgetown. He is on the board of directors at Thomas More College. An accomplished author, Bill has written several books of poetry. His artworks include sketches and drawings of birds, many of which have been exhibited at art shows. Bill is also a proud veteran and is a retired lieutenant serving the United States Naval Reserve.

About the Editor

Paul J. McCarren, S.J. is the author of the *Simple Guides to the Gospels*, four volumes published by Rowman and Littlefield as basic translations and commentaries suitable not only for homilies, but also for high-school scripture courses and parish bible-study groups. McCarren has completed *Simple Guides* for the rest of the New Testament and has begun work on *Guides* for the books of the Old Testament. While writing over the past ten years, he's been leading retreats at the Jesuit Retreat House in Faulkner, Maryland, and doing parish ministry in southern Maryland. From 1974 to 1995, he worked as a professional actor, director, and playwright while also teaching acting courses in Communication Departments at Fordham University, Georgetown University, and Boston College—courses aimed at teaching basic communication skills. From 1996 to 2010 he did parish and campus ministry in Washington, DC. He met Bill Stott in 1974, when they team-taught an acting course at Fordham. They've been pestering one another with their writing projects ever since.

www.ingramcontent.com/pod-product-compliance
Lightning Source LLC
Chambersburg PA
CBHW030524100426
42813CB00001B/139